Dr. J. Harrie

Getting Started With Pet Snakes

From Beginner to Expert Care

First edition

This book was professionally typeset on Reedsy
Find out more at reedsy.com

This book is dedicated to all Snake lovers across the globe.

Contents

1.

2.

3.

4.

5.

6.

7.

8.

9.

10.

11.

12.

13.

Acknowledgement

Special thanks to God, the Publisher, and the Editor for their immense contributions and support in completing this masterpiece.

1

Introduction

Welcome to the exciting world of pet snakes! Whether you're a curious beginner or a seasoned reptile enthusiast, this book is your ultimate guide to understanding, caring for, and nurturing these mesmerizing creatures.

Getting Started With Pet Snakes is more than just a guide – it's a comprehensive and inspiring exploration into the joys and responsibilities of owning a pet snake. We'll cover everything you need to know, from choosing the perfect species and habitat setup, to feeding and breeding, and even common health issues and medical treatments.

With vivid illustrations, and step-by-step instructions, you'll learn how to create a nurturing environment for your snake, build a strong bond, and explore the incredible diversity of these magnificent creatures. From ball pythons to corn snakes, from boas to kingsnakes, each species is unique and fascinating, with its own personality, quirks, and preferences.

So if you're ready to embark on a journey of discovery and adventure, grab your copy of Getting Started With Pet Snakes today! Whether you're a first-time owner or a seasoned pro, this book is the ultimate resource for snake lovers everywhere. Let's dive into the enchanting world of pet snakes together and discover the magic of these slithery, scaly, and utterly   fascinating   creatures.

2

Snakes

Snakes have been enchanting people for millennia. Our culture, literature, and even religion have all been heavily influenced by these beautiful and mysterious creatures. They are available in pretty much every landmass of the world, and every single one of them is one of a kind and delightful in its manner.

We are aware of approximately 3,000 distinct snake species with a variety of sizes, colors, and habitats. There are four families for them: Pythonidae, Colubridae, Elapidae, and Viperidae. These families can also be broken down into a number of genera, each of which has its own characteristics, habitats, and behaviors.

Snakes play a fundamental part in our environment. By eating other animals, like rodents and insects, that could harm crops and other plants, they help maintain the equilibrium of our food chain. They likewise assume a significant role in clinical exploration and assist with creating remedies for wind chomps and venomous diseases.

The structure of snakes' bodies is one of their most fascinating characteristics. They have a long, slim body without any legs, making them exceptionally versatile and quick at traveling through restricted spaces. In addition, snakes have a number of distinct characteristics, such as flexible jaws, forked tongues, and body-covering scales that aid in predator and prey detection.

Snakes have special and profoundly modern senses that empower them to make due in nature. Because of their highly developed senses of taste and smell, they are able to spot prey or predators from a great distance. Winds additionally have exceptionally evolved hearing and vision capacities, which shift contingent upon the species.

Many people are afraid of snakes because of their poisonous nature, despite their beauty and fascination. Even though only a small percentage of snakes are poisonous, if not treated promptly, snake bites can be dangerous and even fatal. The good news is that you can safeguard yourself and stop these deadly incidents from happening if you have a solid understanding of snakes.

We can learn about snake behavior and the characteristics of each species to gain a deeper appreciation for and comprehension of snakes. For instance, the black mamba is known for its deadly speed and agility, while the king cobra is one of the most venomous snakes and can inject venom into your eyes.

Understanding the symbolic meanings that snakes carry in various cultures lends itself to our appreciation of them. For instance, the cobra was revered as a deity in ancient Egyptian culture as a representation of power and royalty. Snakes are revered for their power and mystical abilities in Hinduism, where they are thought to represent divine energies.

All in all, snakes are a significant part of our environment and have been enrapturing people for a really long time. With legitimate information and understanding, we can see the value in their excellence and their part in nature. Snakes have a lot to teach us, and we can all benefit from learning more about them. We can study their behavior, admire their distinctive features, and learn about the symbolism they represent in various cultures.

3

Pet Snakes

Picking a pet snake is totally different from other domesticated animals and sidekick creatures. It's a complicated and risky process. The animals need special care and handling techniques. You need to choose one that is best suited to your handling abilities. Due to their long lifespan, keeping a pet snake can be a long-term commitment.

Most snakes are easy to handle. Even the gentle ones are dangerous. However, the majority of the time, aggressive behavior is triggered by poor living conditions. If you intend to keep a snake and are confident that they will captivate you, you must be committed and sympathetic to their requirements.

Consider the following when considering keeping a pet snake:

1. Snakes have a two-decade lifespan. This is a drawn-out responsibility.
2. Houdini could gain from snakes. They have a remarkable ability to escape. Snakes do not seek freedom; rather, they attain it. It's vital to have a walled-in area that your snake can't outmaneuver.
3. The animal will most likely require live food. While frozen or pre-killed prey is the safest option, live food will keep them interested and active. If you freeze, be ready to store anything in your freezer, including insects, rats, and mice.
4. It is not recommended to keep constricting or venomous snakes, even if they are small, unless you are a skilled handler.

Breeder

Get your pet snake from respectable breeders and sellers. Captured wild snakes will be stressed. They are susceptible to parasites and disease. Taming will be hard because of these characteristics.

In addition, using a reputable breeder or vendor increases your chances of getting a healthy animal. Even if you are not a veterinarian, conduct a cursory inspection before purchasing a snake. Keep an eye out for closed eyes, retained skin, rot in the mouth, and nasal bubbles.

Request a feeding demonstration from the owner. If you choose to feed your desired reptile, you need to know if it likes it and eats well. The ball python, for instance, is known for its difficulty eating and finicky eating habits. Before you get a snake in your home, you want to get rid of it.

Handling Your Pet Snake

You need to adjust the pet to your presence. Furthermore, no proprietor needs a snake they can't hold! However, you want to perform it safely. Young snakes, who aren't used to being touched by humans, will need some training.

First, wash your hands. It's possible to mistake any odor for food. Additionally, cleaning lowers the likelihood of harmful bacteria or parasites being transmitted to the snake. Even though it might not be necessary in the future, you want to get the snake used to people.

Prior to you taking care of your pet, rest your hand in the enclosure for as long as three minutes. At first, the suspicious snake will probably avoid you. In the long run, serious areas of strength for them are smell and remembering you, which will lead them to research.

It takes patience and a calm demeanor to learn to handle a pet snake, which usually costs a lot of money.

Try not to feel that a mitigating discussion might help. Even though they aren't deaf, snakes can't hear what people say. As a result, all you have to do while your hand is in the tank is read a magazine or watch something interesting.

Always move slowly and predictably. Never take a snake by surprise! even if you only look through the window. Straight or sideways approach to your snake, whether it is inside or outside its enclosure. Neither from above nor by surprise.

Still, on the matter of surprises and shocks, abstain from attempting to get a murmuring (hissing) snake. The snake is either defending itself or afraid. After it has eaten, don't mess with it. When it's shed, stay away. When your reptile is awake but still feeling sleepy, it is a good time to   handle   it   until   it   gets   used   to   you.

4

Best Pet Snakes

Snakes are great pets! They are fun and distinctive. There are more than 3,600 species overall, and most of them are versatile for confinement. The following snakes are well-liked and require little care. These are breeds that never grow larger. If you don't like the idea that most breeds eat live food, get a guinea pig. There are options for beginners, experienced players, and kids.

So, here is a list of great pet snakes that are known for being easy to care for, how they act, and how they look.

The Children's Python

This is named after the scientist who described them for the first time in 1842, John George Children, who was the curator of the British Museum's zoological collection at the time of the discovery.

Children's Pythons are uncommon medium-sized snakes that maintain their small size. These pet pythons are gentle enough to be around children under supervision and are great for beginners. For rodents, the reptile requires the most fundamental care and diet. When handled gently and frequently, they have excellent temperaments. They can live for thirty years!

Common Boa Constrictor

Boas are not the best pet for novices due to their enormous size. The boa constrictor, which ranges in length from 13 to 16 feet, requires an experienced handler. The boa, which lives in South and Central America, eats fish, lizards, deer, and other animals. You can feed them chickens, rats, and rabbits as pets. You need to keep them away from kids. Boas are solid and may wrap tight whenever pushed or compromised. The typical BOA costs anywhere from $60 to $200.

Western Hognose Snake

The most distinctive feature of hognose snakes is their upturned snout, which helps them dig in sandy soils by moving side to side.

The Western Hognose Snake, which can be found in the United States, Canada, and Mexico, is characterized by an upturned, pug-like nose. When toads and lizards aren't available, the breeds eat mice and small lizards during the morning and evening hours. To discover toads hidden in the sand, the Hognose digs holes. The hognose is easy to handle, and they don't act aggressively when they hiss. This pet snake costs around $100–$500.

Garter Snake

Garter snakes lack venom and do not have fangs. However, they can bite and have a few rows of small teeth.

Garters are popular house pets and one of the most common wild snakes in the world. Garters in captivity gnaw on small fish and worms. They don't need a lot of maintenance because they need heating and lighting frequently. It's great to set them up with a luxuriating light, as the strap appreciates resting in the sun. They are rare, small snakes because they can only reach a length of four feet. The garter snake is a well-known backyard intruder that is relatively harmless and manageable, making it suitable for children. The snakes cost less than $50, making them affordable.

Ball Python

The ball python gets its name from the way it naturally acts defensively. When they feel threatened, they usually form a ball and put their heads in the middle.

The ball python is popular for its fastidiousness and its food. They prefer meals that have just been thawed or killed, but there are times when they don't eat at all. However, this pet python is docile, calm, and suspicious. The snake's tendency to curl into a ball when threatened is one of its characteristics. They can grow to be thick but only reach a maximum height of five feet. Ball pythons can live for thirty years! This pet python can be purchased for between $25 and $200, depending on its rarity.

California King Snakes (Lampropeltis californiae) are known as kingsnakes because, like the king cobra, they occasionally consume other snakes.

The Cali King Snake typically has yellow bands, stripes, or speckles on its back. The Cali King is an excellent snake for beginners because it is shy and docile when handled frequently. The snake does not scream when it is stressed. The breeds would rather hide and curl up. They require basic care, consume mice, and can live for up to 20 years. One can be yours for anywhere from $70 to $170.

5

Owning a Pet Snake

There are approximately 2,500 distinct snake species. King snakes, rat snakes, garter snakes, corn snakes, various pythons (particularly ball pythons), and various boa constrictors (particularly the common boa constrictor) are among the species that are frequently kept as pets. The requirements of one animal category might contrast from those of another, so make certain to make explicit inquiries with a learned herpetologist (somebody who concentrates on reptiles and creatures of land and water) or a veterinarian acquainted with reptiles. The ball python will be utilized as the emphasis in this chapter, as it is quite possibly one of the most commonly kept pet snakes. The majority of the information about the ball python can be applied to other species of terrestrial snakes.

The majority of snakes sold as pets are manageable and rarely aggressive. Despite the fact that some snake species that are kept by serious reptile collectors are naturally aggressive, they rarely appear in pet stores because they are not common in the pet trade.

After experiencing the stress of moving to a new home and environment, some snakes, particularly the ball python, may not eat for weeks or months. Absence of hunger can be an ordinary response to stretching; however, whenever delayed, it very well might be an indication of a more difficult issue that requires brief veterinary consideration.

After the stress of moving to a new new environment, some snakes, particularly the ball python, may not eat for weeks or months. Ideally, pets should only be purchased from captive-bred animals. Snakes caught in the wild are more likely to refuse food, are less tolerant of stress, and frequently have more internal and external parasites.

Most species of snakes have identical male and female appearances. Using a special instrument, your veterinarian can carefully examine the snake's vent, which opens to the cloaca, to determine your pet's sex.

Because an inexperienced person probing the snake could injure it, snake sexing should only be performed by a trained individual.

Hatchling ball pythons are something like a foot long and develop to around 3 feet by 3 years old. Adults are 5 to 6 feet in length when they reach maturity, which takes 3 to 5 years. Ball pythons can live for 10 to 20 years, depending on how well they are cared for.

What distinguishes snakes from other pets in terms of anatomy?

Scales made of leather cover the snake's skin. Contrary to popular belief, the skin is dry to the touch, smooth, and frequently shiny. Snakes don't have slime. Snakes are ectotherms, which means that their body temperature is determined by the temperature of their environment. As a result, their skin temperature reflects the temperature of the environment, and if the temperature is cold, their skin feels wet.

Instead of eyelids, snakes have spectacles that cover their eyes and keep them open all the time.

Snakes shed their skin like clockwork as they develop. A healthy snake sheds its old skin intact in a healthy environment. Your veterinarian should examine the snake to ensure that there is no underlying infection or issue with inadequate humidity if it does not do so and pieces of old skin remain on the body after shedding.

Snakes, like all reptiles, are ectotherms, which means that they use heat from the outside or the environment to keep themselves warm.

The majority of snakes only have one simple, functional lung, typically the right lung. The other lung is either smaller or absent entirely. The only exception to this rule are pythons and boas, which have two lungs. The muscle that separates the chest and abdomen in mammals is called the diaphragm, but snakes lack it. In order to move air into and out of the lungs, they move the muscles in the ribs and body wall. Between the heart and the hind end, the lung can take up a lot of the snake's body.

Food is swallowed whole by snakes. Vegetarian snakes are not found; carnivores make up every species. The kind of snake they eat determines their diet.

The urinary, digestive, and reproductive tracts of snakes all empty into a cloaca, which is located at the snake's hind end. The cloaca purges externally through the vent tracked down on the snake's underside, at the foundation of the tail. They poo, pee, and repeat through the cloaca.

By carefully embedding a unique test in the cloacal region, a proficient veterinarian can tell the sex of the snake.

Although snakes lack limbs, it has been hypothesized that the two spurs on either side of pythons' and boas' vents are remnants of limbs.

Numerous pairs of ribs run the length of a snake's body. Snakes have three-chambered hearts, while well-evolved creatures and birds have four-chambered hearts.

A snake's diaphragm is absent; they are unable to cough or clear their airways of mucus as a result of this. Thus, snakes with basic respiratory contamination might foster pneumonia.

Just inside the vent, males have two reproductive organs known as hemipenes.

How should I choose a snake?

Most proprietors purchase wind locally from pet stores, despite the fact that mail-ordering from reptile reproducers is additionally normal. On the off chance that you purchase a pet through the mail, ensure you understand what you are getting! It is preferable to view the animal before making a purchase. In the event that the pet does not meet your expectations or is not in good health, inquire about a guarantee. Shelters also accept snakes for adoption.

The best pets are young animals raised in captivity. Older, imported wild-caught animals are more difficult to tame, may have more internal and external parasites, and frequently become ill as a result of the stress of being kept in a cage.

A healthy pet is a good place to start. Avoid snakes that look small or bony, have loose skin, have sunken eyes, or don't move much. Most of the time, a healthy snake is bright, active, and alert. It should be clear to the eyes. The snake may be about to shed if it has cloudy eyes. Although shedding is not a sign of illness, it is extremely stressful for snakes, and during this time, they frequently do not consume any food. A snake that is about to shed should not be purchased. Mites, which look like tiny, moving black dots, can be found under the snake's scales and around its eyes. Verify that the skin does not have any sores or discolorations, as well as any lumps or bumps. You can find any swellings by simply running your hands slowly down the snake's body. The vent ought to be clean and free of any stains or wetness from stools. On the off chance that this is conceivable, tenderly open the mouth. A pink tongue and a small amount of clear saliva should be present. A mouth infection may be indicated by large amounts of mucus that appear cloudy or cottage cheese-like, as well as by red, bloody, or bruised gums.

My snake seems to be fine. Is it really necessary for him to see a vet?

A qualified reptile veterinarian should examine your snake within 48 hours of purchase. The veterinary visit typically includes measuring the animal's weight and looking for signs of external parasites or abnormalities like lumps and bumps. The reptile is inspected for indications of parchedness and unhealthiness. An examination for signs of infection (stomatitis) is performed on the mouth. To check for internal parasites, the feces are subjected to a microscopic examination. Numerous veterinarians think that all snakes (even those reproduced in have digestive parasites and suggest routine antiparasitic treatment. Snakes do not require vaccinations. If the snake appears to be ill, your veterinarian may recommend blood tests, cultures, or X-rays to look for other diseases.

Snakes, like all pets, should be examined at least once a year, and every examination should include a look for parasites in their feces.

6

Housing Your Pet Snake

What kind of cage is necessary for my snake?

You should try to give your snake the biggest cage you can. You need to choose a cage that is suitable for the species' particular requirements. Smaller species or young snakes often do well in an aquarium between 10 and 20 gallons, or even in a plastic Rubbermaid container with airflow holes cut into the top. Your snake must be relocated to a more spacious and comfortable enclosure as it grows. These can be made of plexiglass, glass, fiberglass, or untreated wood by the pet owner or bought from a store. It is important to note that wooden cages are difficult to thoroughly clean and disinfect.

Excrement and dried urates ought to be eliminated every 24-72 hours, and the enclosure ought to be cleaned out week by week. Many individuals endeavor to make a vivarium or terrarium, determined to establish a semi-regular habitat with plants, rocks, and tree limbs. These are much more labor-intensive to maintain, but your pet might be "happier" with them.

"All cages for snakes must be escapeproof, with sealed seams and a locking, secure top." All cages for snakes must be escape-proof with good ventilation. Your veterinarian or pet store might have instances of these bigger, walled-in areas to provide you with an idea of the appropriate territory for a Grown-up snake.

Is bedding necessary for my snake's cage?

The substrate, or bedding material, ought to be nontoxic to the snake and easy to clean. Newspaper, butcher paper, paper towels, or Astroturf (artificial grass) are all good options. Buy two pieces of astroturf and cut them to fit the bottom of the cage when using it. With two pieces, one is kept outside the cage, where it is clean and ready to use, and the other is put inside the cage. You can switch out the dry, clean turf inside the cage as soon as it gets dirty. The soiled turf should be cleaned with regular soap and water (avoid harsher products unless approved by your reptile veterinarian), thoroughly rinsed, and hung to dry before being used for the next cage cleaning.

Keep away from sand, rock, wood shavings, corncob material, pecan shells, and feline litter. In addition to being difficult to clean, these substrates have the potential to impale the intestines if ingested intentionally or unintentionally (if food items become coated in the substrate). Cedar wood shavings are harmful to reptiles and should be avoided!

In the cage, what else do I require?

Normal branches are delighted by the snake. Any normal branch should be liberated from bugs and should not have been in contact with pesticides. Ensure the branches are secure and won't fall onto the snake and harm it. For the snake to bask, the branch should ideally slope from the bottom to the top of the enclosure and end near a heat or light source. Huge rocks can be put in the enclosure to consider relaxing, investigating, and scouring against at the hour of shedding. All reptiles appreciate having a safe place to hide. Clay pots, commercial reptile caves, upside-down boxes, a hollow log, a large piece of curved bark, upside-down boxes, and artificial vegetation are all good places to hide.

Always provide fresh, clean water in a large, heavy ceramic crock or bowl that cannot be easily spilled. A substantial dish may aid in better air humidity maintenance. A few snakes appreciate absorbing this dish occasionally. Numerous snakes drink from and urinate in their water bowls. Water dishes ought to be cleaned and sanitized every 24-72 hours.

What about a heat source?

All reptiles require access to a heat source. As with all reptiles, snakes are ectotherms, or cold-blooded. This indicates that they maintain their body temperature by relying on heat from the outside or the environment. To keep their internal body temperature in check, they need a variety of temperatures. The ideal configuration of the cage would be to create a heat gradient, with one end of the tank being warmer than the other. The snake is able to move around its environment and adjust its body temperature as needed. It is ideal to buy two thermometers (rugged ones that can't be inadvertently gulped) and place one at the cooler end of the enclosure and one at the hotter end, close to the intensity source. You will be able to determine the animal's temperature at that position if you position the thermometer roughly at the height at which it will bask.

The temperature in the cage ought to be comparable to what the animal experiences in its natural, native setting and ought to be representative of the region from which it originates. In general, the warmer end of the cage should be between 90 and 95°F (32 and 38°C), while the cooler end should be between 70 and 75°F (21 and 24°C). A cheap method for doing this is to supply a central intensity source utilizing a 100-watt brilliant bulb with a shielded reflector hood. Then again, you can buy different kinds of intensity lights and infrared intensity producers at specialty pet stores. Utilize these intensity sources as coordinated. In order to keep the snake from escaping or coming into direct contact with the hot bulb, your heat source should be outside the cage, at one end, and covered by a screen. The snake should be able to reach the highest point in the cage, at least 3 to 4 inches away from the heat source. Around evening time, heat isn't required, as long as the temperature stays at 65–70 oF (18–21 oC).

"Hot Shakes" or "Sizzle Rocks" are hazardous, can prompt injury, are insufficient, and ought to be stayed away from."

Human-grade warming cushions or under-tank heat cushions underneath the enclosure can likewise be utilized for warmth. If it's not too much trouble, talk with your veterinarian to gain proficiency with the right method for utilizing them, assuming that you pick this type of warming. "Hot Rocks" or "Sizzle Rocks" are dangerous, ineffective, and can cause injury; they should not be used!

The required natural humidity varies by region and season. For snakes, some homes are too dry. Many snakes do well with humidity levels between 40% and 70%, depending on the species. Additionally, excessive humidity can be harmful and cause health issues. It is evident that desert species require less humidity.

What about light with UVB?

There is a lack of knowledge regarding snakes' requirements for light. While most reptiles require UV-B light to make vitamin D3, veterinarians disagree about whether snakes require UV light. This is because snakes eat whole prey, which has a good balance of nutrients for snakes. However, providing UV light would certainly not be harmful and may even be beneficial, so providing a Vita-Lite or other UV-B light would probably be prudent. Talk with your nearby pet store or your veterinarian about the requirement for UV–B light for your snake. In an effort to improve health, balance, and breeding success, a lot of people try to imitate the natural seasonal change in light, also known as the photoperiod.

7

Feeding Pet Snakes

Carnivores make up all snakes. Their eating routine depends on the species. Others consume insects, amphibians (such as frogs or toads), eggs, other reptiles, fish, earthworms, or slugs, while others consume warm-blooded prey (such as rodents, rabbits, or birds). Snakes gulp down their food. The most popular snakes for pets typically consume rodents, such as rats, gerbils, and hamsters. Rabbits are also eaten whole by larger pet snakes.

Since snakes eat whole prey, it is more straightforward for their proprietors to take care of them healthfully and complete weight control plans, which absolutely forestalls a considerable number of the dietary-related sicknesses normally seen in different reptiles. A snake can get a complete and balanced diet from whole prey like mice and rats. However, some people find it difficult to feed reptiles their whole prey. Even though rodents are now commercially available already dead and frozen, all you need to do to offer them to your snake is thaw them. If you are squeamish about feeding them, a snake probably isn't the right pet for you!

Snakes should not be fed live prey. Live prey ought not be taken care of by snakes, as the prey won't just experience mental pressure while being pursued by the snake but additionally take steps to hurt the snake by gnawing it before they are eaten. A pet snake can be seriously injured by a bite from a small mouse, which can result in a severe, potentially fatal infection.

Train your pet snake to consume dead prey. Snakes can be offered either defrosted, recently frozen prey, or freshly killed ones.

How frequently would it be advisable for me to feed my snake?

That all depends on the age, size, and activity level of your snake. More modest or more youthful snakes, for the most part, eat two times every week, while bigger, more adult snakes commonly eat once consistently or two. Feeding frequency can be increased for female snakes that are getting ready to breed. Depending on your snake's specific needs, your veterinarian can provide you with more specific feeding recommendations. When you give your pet food, he will respond by telling you how often he needs to eat. He was hungry and would require food if he ate. If he doesn't eat it right away, he probably wasn't hungry and didn't need to be fed yet.

My snake refuses to eat! What's going on?

There are many reasons for a pet snake not having any desire to eat, from harmless causes, for example, the pressure of being in a new or upset climate, commotion, absence of security, ill-advised ecological temperature, hibernation, shedding, pregnancy, or rearing season anorexia, to additional serious goals, including malignant growth, kidney disappointment, parasites, or other medical problems. Through a comprehensive physical examination and appropriate laboratory testing, your veterinarian can assist in determining the cause of your snake's decreased appetite.

Do I have to provide vitamins to my snake?

Generally speaking, no. However, due to the fact that your snake "is what he eats," it is essential to ensure that your snake's prey is well-fed and healthy. Because of this, some snake owners, particularly collectors, raise their own rodents for their snakes to eat.

What about water?

Always provide a large, heavy ceramic crock or bowl containing clean, fresh water that cannot be easily spilled. A substantial dish may assist in maintaining the tank's necessary humidity levels, which are essential for keeping the snake hydrated and facilitating its proper shed. Since some snakes also like to periodically soak in their water dish, the dish should be large enough to accommodate that. Change the water frequently and wash, disinfect, and rinse the water bowl every day because many snakes will   eat   and   drink   from   it.

8

Breeding Your Pet Snakes

Although the process by which various species of snake reproduce varies, there are some fundamental measures you should take to ensure your snake's health before and during reproduction.

Give your pet snake the right amount of heat to get it ready for breeding. In most cases, snakes are content with temperatures between 85 and 100 degrees Fahrenheit. Also, try not to handle your snake after it has eaten, because doing so might make it eat again.

Create a hibernation facility. Depending on the kind of snake you have, hibernation may be a crucial component for successful breeding. You'll need to give your snake the separation of a hibernation chamber. To make one, find a crate that is somewhat smaller than your snake's enclosure. Corncob bedding or another type of similar bedding can be used to fill it up to ten inches deep. This is where your snake will burrow. In addition, you'll want to ensure that the temperature in this chamber stays consistent between 55 and 60 degrees Fahrenheit.

Into hibernation: To set up your snake for hibernation, assess your female's wellbeing with the assistance of your snake's veterinarian. In the week leading up to hibernation, you should give your snake warm baths on a daily basis. This will assist with eliminating waste from your snake's body. The temperature in your snake's cage should gradually decrease. Make sure to bring your snake into the hibernation chamber with a bowl of water as well. Keep your snake there for eight weeks, then give it water whenever it's needed. After eight weeks, start raising the temperature in the hibernation chamber until it reaches the living quarters' normal range. You can then return the snake to its usual cage.

Bringing the two together: You should now move your female into the male's cage. By reading her body language, you can determine her willingness to reproduce. She is prepared if she lies down and appears to be at ease near the male. Repeat the process of reintroducing your snakes every few days until the female appears to have lost interest in the male. At this point, she will begin producing eggs. You only have to wait for her to conceive or give birth to live children after this. The average gestational age is between 28 and 45 days.

Even though there may be a few steps, some of which take time, there is a good chance that you will produce children that you can either sell or raise on your own!

9

Caring for Your Pet Snake

Snakes make wonderful pets. They are quiet, clean, and don't need to be walked or talked to often. Additionally, for safe handling and care, they only require a small amount of specialized equipment.

Habitat

It is impossible to generalize about snake care. Research the species to obtain specific information on how to properly care for your pet, because some species require specialized handling. Ask your pet retailer for your snake's particular ecological prerequisites.

It is necessary to replicate your snake's natural environment as closely as possible in order to provide the best care for it. The best enclosures for your snake are habitat aquariums or terrariums with integrated screen covers or enclosures made of high-density plastic (HDPE or PVC) designed for reptiles. They will provide the heat that cold-blooded animals need, and they will also allow for adequate ventilation and visibility.

Snakes use both horizontal and vertical surfaces, so their enclosure ought to give them enough room to stretch out and move around freely. A nook that is longer and more profound than it is tall is preferred, except if you are wanting to keep an arboreal species that requires a level for climbing. Snakes may injure their face or skin by striking or rubbing against the side walls of an enclosure that has wire because of this.

Security-oriented screen covers are a must. Check to see that the locking system in the enclosure is adequate. Snakes can open doors and squeeze through small gaps like escape artists. Snakes should be kept alone, unlike the majority of other reptile pets.

As long as it fulfills a few fundamental requirements, the interior of your snake's home can be as straightforward or as complex as you like. Regardless of the species, a perfect climate with proper temperature and moisture is the main factor in keeping a sound snake. Indeed, even water snakes, support snakes, and different species from high-moisture environments should include a dry space inside the nook.

A newspaper substrate, a substantial water dish big enough for drinking and soaking, and a hiding place can all make up a basic enclosure. You can create a natural environment by adding cypress bark, grapevine branches, driftwood, hollowed cholla branches, aspen shavings, silica sand, stones and rocks, or dry leaves, depending on the species of snake you've chosen. While burrowing species use potting soil or leaf litter, desert species prefer sand. Toxic cedar wood and shavings should be avoided.

It is critical to incorporate a concealing spot in the nook. Snakes enjoy curling up in a tight hiding spot that may appear to be just big enough for them.

Water

It is important to have fresh water in a heavy, shallow water dish for drinking and soaking. On the off chance that your dish isn't huge enough for the snake to totally lower itself, utilize a unique plastic holder week after week so your pet can move about, splash, unwind, shed its skin, or ease itself if vital. Some tropical and small species like to drink from spray bottles that create artificial rain. Change the water and clean the dish consistently.

Diet

All snakes are flesh-eating. In bondage, they normally eat mice, rodents, chicks, fish, eggs, red worms, and crickets. It is possible to train most snake species to eat rodents instead of amphibians, reptiles, or birds. The kind of food and how frequently you feed will change depending on the species, age of the snake, and season. Snakes typically require food once every one to two weeks.

Your snake's jaw can expand, allowing it to eat a rodent that is bigger than its head. However, it should never eat anything that is much wider than the snake's thickest point. Frozen rodents should be fed whenever possible. They are safer and healthier than live rodents, which could bite your snake in self-defense. Additionally, the freezing process will have eradicated the majority of internal or external parasites that the prey item may carry. Rodents should not be thawed in areas where humans prepare food.

Temperature and Humidity

Snakes need a temperature slope of 10–15 °F across their living space. A warming cushion put under the floor toward one side of the nook ought to be adequate to give a warm region, while a concealing spot in the cooler corner permits your snake to look for the temperature it wants. Glowing reptile light installations with a spotlight or ceramic radiator are a possibility for keeping up with the suitable temperature.

The amount of humidity required by a species varies, with tropical species like Boa constrictors from Central and South America requiring 50–60% and desert species like Sand Boas from northern Africa requiring 10–30%. The majority of snakes have adequate humidity requirements in their water dish. On the off chance that your environment is extremely dry, utilize a splash jug to fog the territory; incidentally, try not to douse the substrate, which can prompt parasites and medical conditions.

Each day, snakes should get several hours of natural light. Unless your snake's natural habitat lacks sunlight, ultraviolet (UV-B) lights are unnecessary.

Handling

To avoid startling your snake, ensure that it is awake before removing it from its environment (snakes do not have eyelids to close while they are sleeping). It's critical to let your snake know when it's time to handle it and when it's time to feed it. You can achieve this by tenderly moving the snake with an item, for example, a snake snare.

When the snake is aware of your presence and isn't hoping to be taken care of, you might get it by tenderly getting a handle on it mid-body with two hands and supporting as much of its length across your hands and arms as could be expected. To prevent the snake from entering small spaces, it is essential to always be aware of where its head is. Keep an eye out for any indications that your snake is acting out and should be returned to its natural habitat. When handling specimens that are longer than six feet, more than one person should be involved. Without the supervision of an adult, minors should not handle snakes.

Health

Maintaining good health for both you and your snake will help keep your pets healthy and reduce the likelihood that your snake will spread disease to humans. Keep your pet's health in check by taking the following measures, in addition to providing the appropriate diet, temperature, and humidity:

Daily, spot clean the enclosure and remove animal waste.

Cleaning the rocks and branches thoroughly, turning the substrate, getting rid of any large clumps, and wiping down the glass should all be part of the weekly maintenance routine.

Snakes ought to be maneuvered carefully under grown-up management. A snake may be startled by sudden movements, which may cause it to strike defensively, causing serious injury. After handling your snake, it is always essential to wash your hands with antibacterial soap.

Disinfect and clean all bottles, bowls, and dishes on a weekly basis.

10

Common Diseases of Pet Snakes

Infectious stomatitis, also known as mouth rot, parasites (including cryptosporidiosis), skin infections, inclusion body disease, respiratory disease, and septicemia are all conditions that frequently affect pet snakes.

An infection of the mouth known as infectious stomatitis, also known as "mouth rot," manifests itself in the form of small hemorrhages on the gums or an excessive amount of thick mucus in the mouth and at the inside edge of the front of the mouth that looks like cottage cheese or contains blood. In extreme cases, the snake has a seriously enlarged mouth, is open-mouth breathing, and isn't eating. This issue may not be an essential sickness but rather be optional to a physical issue in the mouth or to farming issues like unfortunate nourishment, inappropriate natural temperature, mugginess, or congestion.

Both interior parasites (different worms and coccidia) and outside parasites (ticks and bugs) are normal in pet snakes. They are typically found during a yearly physical examination and fecal tests, but they rarely cause obvious symptoms. They may, notwithstanding, cause runs, breathing troubles, disgorging, expanding of inside organs, tingling, skin disturbance, weakness, mouth disease (bugs can send the microbes that cause contamination), and weight reduction. A protozoal parasite known as cryptosporidiosis is capable of infecting snakes and causing weight loss, impaired digestion, vomiting, and thickening of the stomach muscles—which can be seen from the outside of the snake as a round, mid-body swelling. Some snakes have the infection, but they don't show any symptoms. Instead, they release the contagious parasite in their feces, making other snakes more likely to get it.

Skin disease (dermatitis) is in many cases found in snakes (and different reptiles) kept in conditions that are excessively wet as well as grimy. Snakes may have red, inflamed skin with numerous small, blister-like lesions on the snake's underside, making it easy to miss them. If not treated promptly, these fluid-filled blisters may progress to severe skin damage, septicemia (a blood infection caused by bacteria), and death. Snakes that are kept in conditions that are too dry and don't have enough humidity may retain skin when they shed and get bacterial infections of the skin from debris that builds up under the skin that is retained.

A very serious viral disease that affects boas and pythons is called inclusion body disease (IBD). Boas may carry this virus for more than a year without showing any obvious signs of infection, in contrast to pythons, which typically exhibit symptoms of infection. The symptoms vary widely. Although it can affect the digestive or respiratory systems, this disease usually affects the nervous system. When affected snakes are placed on their backs, they are unable to stand up, may appear to be "star gazing," and may even become paralyzed. IBD is usually fatal and spreads from snake to snake.

Snakes have a special way of breathing. The majority of snakes only have one simple, functional lung, typically the right lung; the left one is diminished in size or totally missingis diminished in size or totally missing. Boas and pythons are the special cases for this, with two lungs. Snakes lack a diaphragm muscle that separates their abdominal cavity from their chest cavity. To move air into and out of the lungs, they rely on the rib and body wall muscles. Between the heart and the hind end, the lung can take up a lot of the snake's body.

The majority of snake respiratory infections are brought on by bacteria and can occur concurrently with stomatitis. Diseases of the respiratory tract can also be caused by parasites, fungi, and viruses. Snakes with respiratory diseases might have an overabundance of bodily fluid in their mouths, nasal release, dormancy, loss of hunger, wheezing, and may make 'murmuring' sounds or open their mouths to relax.

"The majority of snake respiratory infections are caused by bacteria and may occur concurrently with mouth rot."

Bacteria and the toxins they produce proliferate in the blood stream and other body organs in septicemia. Septicemia affects snakes severely and frequently puts them on the verge of death. They often have a red discoloration on the scales of their bellies and exhibit lethargy, a lack of appetite, and breathing with their mouths open.

What signs does my snake have of illness?

Snake disease symptoms can be specific to a specific disease, like a cottage cheese-like discharge in the mouth of a snake with stomatitis, or they can be non-specific, like a lack of appetite and lethargy, which are signs of many diseases. Your veterinarian should assess your pet as soon as possible if there is any deviation from normal.

How are snake-borne illnesses treated?

Treatment for infectious stomatitis typically involves rinsing the mouth with antibiotic solutions and injecting antibiotics.

snakes-sicknesses 2 For parasitic contamination, deworming prescriptions are given to the snake either orally or through infusion. The medication required is determined by the type of parasite found. Some parasitic issues, like cryptosporidiosis, may be difficult to treat, if not impossible.

Dermatitis can be cured with a legitimate climate and cleanliness. If this disease has progressed, oral and injectable antibiotics, as well as topical treatment, are required.

Since there is no treatment for inclusion body disease, most snakes are euthanized. New animals must be strictly quarantined, and pythons and boas should be housed separately to prevent seemingly normal boas carrying this potentially fatal infection from spreading to more vulnerable pythons.

Respiratory contaminations in snakes are most frequently caused by microbes, but in addition, different life forms might be expected, including parasites, growths, and infections. Snakes can occasionally produce nasal discharge as a result of environmental irritants. In order to determine the source of the infection, your veterinarian may suggest nasal or oral discharge cultures, blood tests, or X-rays. Treatment of respiratory illness includes oral or injectable anti-toxins and sporadic nose or eye drops. In the hospital, severely ill snakes require intensive care, which includes fluid therapy and force feeding.

Septicemia is a true emergency that necessitates prompt hospital treatment. In an effort to save the snake, antibiotics, fluid therapy, and force feeding are required.

Any of these conditions can be severe enough to cause sluggishness and a lack of appetite. If your pet snake behaves abnormally, see a veterinarian right away.

11

Common Problems of Pet Snakes

Snakes have a few remarkable issues, and understanding these issues will permit you to more readily focus on your pet and limit future medical service issues.

Anorexia

Anorexia refers to a refusal or lack of appetite. Anorexia is a common condition in snakes, with some species more susceptible than others. Anorexia can occur naturally during reproduction (the breeding season), egg production (a pregnant snake), or shedding. Anorexia can also be a sign of an underlying environmental issue, such as a bad light cycle, a bad diet, eating food in the wrong size, or, most commonly, the stress of a new or different environment.

Anorexia is a common symptom in snakes, with some species more susceptible than others. Infectious stomatitis (also known as "mouth rot"), internal parasites, gastrointestinal blockages (also known as "impactions"), intestinal infections, respiratory conditions, kidney or liver failure, tumors, and gout are among the conditions that can lead to anorexia. Your veterinarian should carry out a careful actual assessment and run lab tests to determine the reason for a snake's anorexia. It can be difficult to get an anorexic snake to eat again, but it will work best if the underlying cause of the anorexia can be found and addressed.

Salmonella

Despite the fact that snakes and other reptiles can carry these bacteria as part of their normal gastrointestinal bacterial flora, turtles are the most frequently implicated in the transmission of Salmonella bacteria to their owners. Salmonella can result in life-threatening septicemia or severe gastrointestinal disease. Despite the fact that they shed the bacteria in their feces and serve as a source of infection for others, many animals and humans carry these bacteria without showing any clinical signs.

Hygiene is the best way to prevent this disease from causing problems. When the snake's cage becomes soiled, thoroughly clean and disinfect it. After using cleaning products, thoroughly rinse the entire cage after disinfecting it at least once per week. Most importantly, after handling, feeding, or cleaning your snake's cage, thoroughly wash and disinfect your hands.

Whenever the snake's cage becomes soiled, thoroughly clean and disinfect it.

The majority of snakes that carry Salmonella are usually healthy and do not require treatment.

Swellings and Masses that are Abnormal

Snakes frequently develop masses and lumps, either on their bodies or on their skin. Different circumstances can cause these unusual swellings and masses. Tumors, parasites, or infections can all result in external lumps. These conditions are typically referred to as abscesses. Organ enlargement (such as kidney disease or stomach parasitic infections), retained eggs from snake species that lay eggs, tumors, or even constipation can all result in internal swellings. A lump may simply be the food that a snake has consumed recently.

In order to determine the cause of a particular swelling, your veterinarian may need to perform certain tests, such as X-rays, aspirations, or blood tests. Your veterinarian will decide whether medical or surgical therapy is the best course of action once the cause of the swelling has been identified. Some bumps and lumps are harmless and do not threaten your snake's life. Other symptoms may indicate a more serious illness. The sooner your snake is examined in these situations, the better.

Difficulty shedding

In the process of ecdysis, a healthy snake will shed its skin in one piece, like an inverted sock. The recurrence of shedding differs with the snake's age, development rate, and nutritional status. A young, well-fed snake will shed more frequently (maybe every month). The first sign of shearing is a subtle dulling of the skin's color throughout the body. After a few days, the eyes turn a cloudy, blue-grey color. The eyes clear and regain their normal appearance as the skin color brightens. Snakes should be handled with extreme caution during these stages because their skin is fragile and susceptible to damage. The snake finally looks for a rough surface to rub against, and as it rubs, the old skin falls off from head to tail. The entire procedure can take anywhere from seven to fourteen days.

Dysecdysis, or difficulty or improper shedding, occurs in some snakes.

Dysecdysis, or difficulty or improper shedding, occurs in some snakes. Dysecdysis is thought to be a sign of a deeper issue, usually with management and husbandry, like low humidity or temperature levels in the environment or inadequate nutrition. The snake with retained eyeglasses is of particular concern. The surfaces of the eyes ought to be shed simultaneously with the skin Dysecdysis is thought to be a sign of a deeper issue, usually with management and husbandry, like low humidity or temperature levels in the environment or inadequate nutrition. The snake with retained eyeglasses is of particular concern. The surfaces of the eyes ought to be shed simultaneously with the skin. Make sure the spectacles are removed with the rest of the skin by checking the shed skin regularly. If they do not shed, you should talk to your veterinarian about the best treatment for your snake. Retiring glasses can lead to permanent eye damage and blindness in the long run.

Increased humidity in the snake's environment can often be used to treat shedding issues like retained skin and eye caps by encouraging the snake to shed the skin. It is essential to provide the snake with a sufficient number of rough surfaces, such as logs or rocks, on which it can rub to initiate the shed. In order to ensure that your pet snake does not suffer any long-term harm, you should seek advice from your veterinarian regarding a variety of methods, such as soaking or misting the snake, to increase the humidity and facilitate the shedding of retained skin and eye caps.

Burns

With pet snakes, burns occur all too frequently. They happen when an animal, naturally looking for a warm place to rest, finds one that's too hot or stays in that hot place for too long. This may occur if the snake has access to electric "hot rocks" or "sizzle stones" or exposed heat lamps, light bulbs, or both within the cage. It can likewise work out in the event that your snake escapes and tracks down a radiator, baseboard warmer, light, or other uncovered heat source on which to sit. When snakes come into contact with hot surfaces, they typically do not realize that they are getting too hot. As a result, they frequently get burned, and some of those burns can be severe. The snake's scales will turn a dark brown or black color with less severe burns; blisters or deep tissue damage will appear in more severe cases. These creatures need prompt veterinary consideration.

Bites and Wounds

The majority of snake owners are surprised to learn that even a small, terrified mouse offered as prey to a snake can severely bite the snake and injure it, putting the snake's life in danger if the snake is not hungry. Predator wounds to reptiles necessitate immediate medical attention. When left in a cage with a well-fed snake, unfinished prey can occasionally inflict injuries that are either irreparable or life-threatening by biting through the skin and muscles all the way down to the ribs and backbone. Hence, as well as accommodating concerns for live prey, snakes ought to be offered just dead (newly killed or frozen and defrosted) prey. Offering live prey simply presents a lot of hazard for injury to the snake, so it ought to be kept away from through and through. The majority of pet snakes can be trained to consume freshly killed and warm dead prey, especially if the snake is hungry.

Injuries

Nasal or facial injuries from superficial skin and scale damage to deep, full-thickness ulceration that can result in nose and front of the mouth deformities that make it difficult to breathe or eat. It is challenging to prevent this issue. If your snake keeps trying to get out, give it a lot of safe places to hide and climb, and put a decorative facade, dark-colored paint, duct tape, or other visual barrier on the outside of the tank walls or on top of the enclosure to keep it from trying to get out.

Dystocia

Egg binding, also known as dystocia, occurs when the female snake is unable to lay eggs. Dystocia is a potentially fatal condition that affects a lot of reptiles. Poor husbandry, such as inadequate lighting or temperature in the environment, a poor nesting location, an inappropriate diet (malnutrition), and dehydration, are among the causes.

Different variables that might contribute to dystocia include more established age, unfortunate body conditions, actual impediments inside the conceptive parcel brought about by twisted or larger than usual eggs or wounds, primary anomalies with the regenerative plot or pelvis, contaminations, clogging, or abscesses. While a healthy gravid (with eggs) snake should be bright, active, and alert, it should not eat. A gravid snake with dystocia won't eat and won't move, be weak, or respond to anything. Snakes in this condition should be examined right away by a veterinarian who is familiar with reptiles. Diagnostic procedures frequently include a physical examination, blood tests, and radiographs (X-rays). To treat these animals, medical or surgical procedures may be required.

12

Veterinary Care

Discovering that all pets, including reptiles, require an initial physical examination by a reptile veterinarian and at least an annual checkup surprises many reptile owners. In fact, a number of reptile veterinarians suggest having checkups at least twice a year to allow for the early detection and treatment of diseases that could be fatal.

After you get your pet reptile, the first visit is the most important one.

Standard veterinary consideration is fundamental to guaranteeing your pet a long, solid life. The very first visit, following the acquisition of your pet reptile, is the most crucial one. The veterinarian will check your pet's health and look for signs of disease during this visit by performing a physical exam and diagnostic tests. A thorough discussion of how to feed, house, and take care of your new pet will be part of the visit. It's critical that you trust your veterinarian and the staff at the hospital and feel at ease with them. Make sure the vet who takes care of your pet is trained and experienced in treating reptiles.

Since reptile medicine is now a subspecialty of veterinary medicine, many general practitioners of dogs and cats are unfamiliar with it. Inquire about your veterinarian's credentials, which ought to include membership in good standing in the ARAV (Association of Reptile and Amphibian Veterinarians). On the off chance that they are not happy seeing your pet, request that they refer you to somebody who has more insight.

Parts of the Reptile Checkup

While each veterinarian has its own set of guidelines for how to examine a new reptile, all veterinarians will carry out or recommend certain tests to help ensure your new pet's health. Some reptile veterinarians recommend injectable sedatives or short-acting gas anesthesia for sedation, depending on the reptile species involved, the test, and/or your pet's temperament. Blood samples from aggressive snakes, lizards, and very large tortoises frequently require sedation. Sedated pets are less likely to be stressed, which is known to be a factor in the deaths of some sick reptiles when handled. If your pet is easily stressed, performing diagnostic procedures under sedation may also be easier and safer.

An examination of the body

Each visit begins with a careful assessment. The Vet will take notes about your pet's weight, general appearance, and mobility during the physical exam. Your veterinarian will audit any data that you might have been given when you obtained your new reptile and will talk about the pet's dietary requirements and general considerations. Then, at that point, the veterinarian will touch or feel different pieces of the pet's body. The need for specialized testing may be indicated by any observed abnormalities.

A blood test

Similarly, as your own normal clinical visit incorporates blood testing, so does a standard exam for pets. A complete blood count, which looks at platelets, red blood cells, and platelets, and a serum biochemical profile, which looks at internal organ function and electrolytes, are two types of blood tests.

Waste Investigation

Intestinal parasites like coccidia, protozoa, and/or intestinal worms can be seen during a microscopic examination of the feces.

Testing for microbes

Unique stains, called Gram stains, might be utilized on waste swabs, skin scrapings, or other examples to identify the presence of strange microorganisms and yeasts. Additional tests like a culture and sensitivity may be suggested based on the results of the Gram stains.

Skin Scratching

A skin scraping may also be taken by your veterinarian to check for mites that burrow under the scales.

Tests using radioactivity

Your pet's body can be examined for abnormalities in the size, shape, and position of organs using radiographs (x-rays), as well as for masses like tumors, granulomas, or enlarged organs. Radiographs likewise consider the identification of unusual liquid gatherings and give an extraordinary visual evaluation of bone and joint construction.

13

Conclusion

As you close the final pages of Getting Started With Pet Snakes, take a deep breath and let it out slowly. Congratulations! You have just completed a journey that will forever change the way you view these amazing creatures. Whether you are now a devoted snake enthusiast or just a little less scared of them, the information in this book has provided you with the knowledge you need to make informed decisions about snakes and their role in our ecosystem. From their beautiful colors and unique patterns to their incredible adaptations, we hope that you have gained a newfound respect for these often-misunderstood animals. Remember, knowledge is the key to overcoming our fears, and with the knowledge you have gained in this book, you can confidently navigate the world of snakes. So go ahead, take that next step, and venture out to discover more about these fascinating creatures. Happy exploring!

Printed in Great Britain
by Amazon